# OCEAN LIFE

Theresa Greenaway

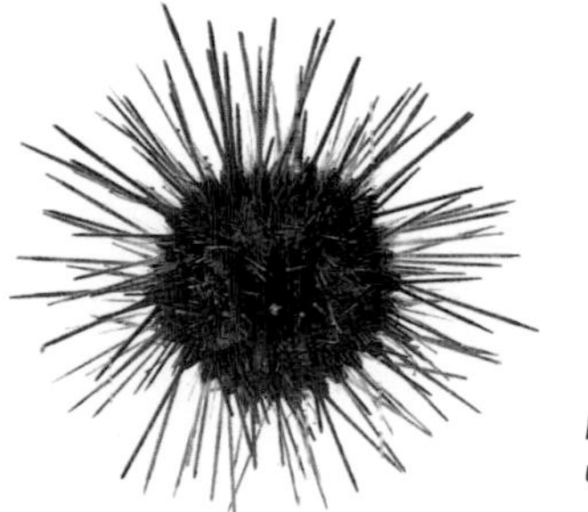

*Hatpin urchin*

A Golden Photo Guide from St. Martin's Press

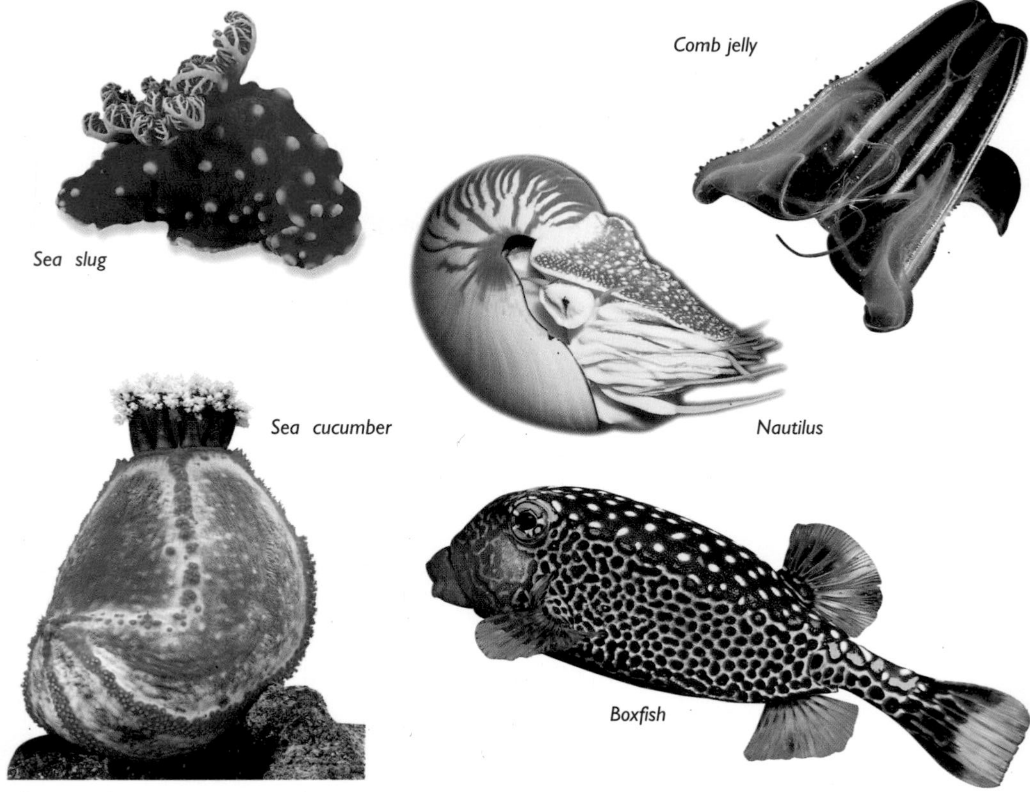
Sea slug
Comb jelly
Nautilus
Sea cucumber
Boxfish

# OCEAN LIFE

## A Golden Photo Guide from St. Martin's Press

*Firebrick starfish*

St. Martin's Press
New York

Manufactured in China

Produced by
Elm Grove Books Limited
**Series Editor** Susie Elwes
**Text Editor** Angela Wilkes
**Art Director** Susi Martin
**Index** Hilary Bird
**Picture Research**
Cathie Arrington
**Consultants**
Martin & Heather Angel



**St. Martin's Press**
**175 Fifth Avenue**
**New York N.Y.10010.**
**www.stmartins.com**

A CIP catalogue record for this book is available from the Library of Congress

ISBN 1-58238-180-1



Text and Photographs in this book previously published in *Eyewitness 3D Ocean Life*

This edition published 2001

---

**ACKNOWLEDGMENTS**
**Heather Angel**: 7br, 13bl, 16bc, 30 bl, 31br, 41bc; **Ardea** 16tl; **Mark Blum**: 7c, 11c, 14c, 30c, 35tl, 36c 38c, 40c, 42c, 48c, 50tl, **Ryan Boerma** 51tl 52tl; BBC Natural History Unit: 18l; **Clay Bryce**: 25c, 36bc, 52b; **Bruce Coleman** : 6r, 8tl, 9r, 21bl, 29tl, 29bl, 29br, 32bc, 33cl, 34, 35c, 38c, 44, 45tl, 45cr, 47c; **Mark Coulin** 19br, **R Davies for Dorling Kindersley** 26-27 b; **Frank Lane Picture Agency**: 7tr, 13tl, 23lr, 28tl, 41tl, 49br, 51bl; **Tim Hellier**: 30br; **NHPA**: 5C, 5tl, 6br, 6r, 10r, 11l, 11bc, 15br, 33bl, 37r, 40r, 42, 48br, 39br, 42c, 48bc, 51r, 53bl; **Oxford Scientific Films**: 5r, 15bl, 17bl, 17br, 20r, 22l, 24tl, 28bl, 31tl, 32tr, 33br, 39tl, 45r; **Christopher Parks:** 9c, 13bl, 21c, 22r, 23br, 26tl, 29c 48r; **Peter Parks**: 13c, 23c, 33c, 51; **Planet Earth**: 8bl, 9bc, 12r, 12l, 14l, 17tl, 19tl,19bl, 20bc, 21tl, 46r, 46l, 47r, 47l, 49bl, 53tr, 53br; **Still Pictures** 15r, 41r, 53; **Tony Stone** 7l, 9tl, 10, 11lr, 14r, 21br, 24bl, 26tl, 50b; **Wim van Egmond**: 17c; **Louisa Wood** 4,5c

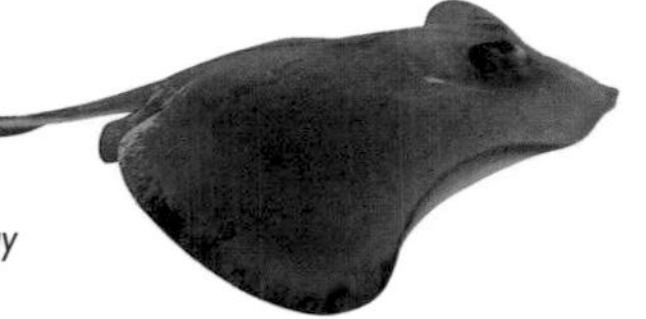
Stingray

# CONTENTS



Sea anemone

# OCEANS AND SEAS

*Stagshorn and brain corals are growing on this wreck. Eventually it will be completely covered by a coral reef.*

Seawater covers 71 percent of the surface of the Earth. The top levels of the oceans teem with an amazing variety of life. Shallow coastal waters ebb and flow with the daily tides. Away from the coast, the seabed plunges ever deeper in an underwater landscape of plains, mountains, and valleys. The sun lights the upper layers, but below 3280 ft (1000 m) the water is totally dark. The surface of the sea freezes in polar regions and is warm in the tropics.

## SEA PEN

A sea pen, anchors itself to a rock and sieves the water for food.

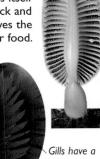

*Gills have a large surface area.*

## GILLS

Sea animals breathe oxygen dissolved in seawater passing through their gills.

## FISHY PAST

Life has been evolving in the sea for over 500 million years. This John Dory is one of the thousands of different species of fish living in the marine environment today.

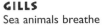

## WRECK SCENE

When a wreck sinks in warm, shallow water, it is soon colonized by corals. Schools of fish, like these French grunts, make the wreck their home.

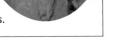

## CHIMNEY

Deep on the ocean floor there are cracks where the earth's crust has moved. Hot, mineral-rich springs spurt up through these cracks like black smoke. As the water cools, the minerals solidify. Eventually, they make tall chimneys.

# BETWEEN THE TIDES

On most seashores, the tidal waters come in and go out twice a day. This movement of seawater is caused by the gravitational pull of the moon and, to a lesser extent, that of the sun. When the tide goes out, sand, pebbles, rocks, and all the seaweeds and animals living on them are exposed to the air. They have to survive hot, dry sunshine as well as winds that dry them out.

### BUTTERFISH

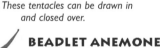

The slippery butterfish lies hidden below the seaweed among rocks at low tide. It disappears into a dark rock crevice if it is disturbed.

### COMMON PRAWN

Perfectly camouflaged at the bottom of a rock pool the common prawn is invisible until it moves.

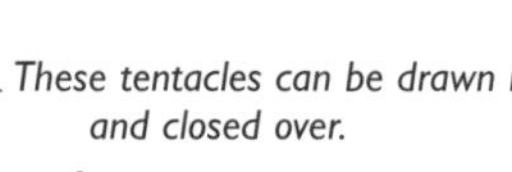

*These tentacles can be drawn in and closed over.*

### BEADLET ANEMONE

Rock pools left by the tide are a safe home for many sea animals, such as beadlet anemones. When they are exposed to the air, they contract into a jellylike blob.

## ROCK CREVICE

In rock pools small animals and seaweeds stay covered by water when the tide goes out. Rock crevices in deep water protect some species found in rock pools such as anemones, but also shelter sea slugs, which live in deep water.

Anemone

Hilton's sea slug

## PRICKLY COCKLE

A prickly cockle lives buried in the sand at the low tide level. It filters food from seawater.

Each periwinkle retreats into a thick yellow, green, or brown shell when it is exposed to the air.

## BAT STARS

These short-armed starfish are all the same species, although they are different colors. They feed on both sea animals and seaweeds.

## SURVIVAL TACTICS.

The leathery fronds of bladder wrack are covered with a slimy layer of mucus that keeps them from drying out at low tide. Periwinkles hide among the damp fronds until the tide comes in.

# SHALLOW WATERS

**COMMON WHELK**
This mollusk lives in shallow, coastal waters with sandy or muddy seabeds. Its thick shell often becomes encrusted with small sponges.

In shallow coastal waters where the water is clear, sunlight reaches right down to the seabed. The seaweed and animals that live here are never uncovered by tides, but the water warms up and cools down faster than it does farther out to sea. Food is plentiful. Small animals feed on bits of seaweed that have been broken up by waves on the shore. Larger animals feast on the smaller ones.

**FAST AND FLAT**
Flatfish such as this flounder lie buried in the sand, waiting for small sea animals to come close enough to catch. A flounder's strange shape does not prevent it from swimming fast when it is disturbed.

*A newly hatched flounder is fish-shaped, but as it grows, the eye on its right side moves onto the left side, which becomes the upper side of the adult fish.*

## SAND DOLLARS

When alive, these flattened sea urchins are buried just beneath the sand. They feed on tiny pieces of dead seaweed and animals.

## PAINTED ROCK LOBSTER

This colorful lobster grows up to 18.5 in (46 cm) long. It lives in the warm, shallow waters of tropical lagoons. At night, it scavenges for food on the seabed.

*These eyes are constantly on the lookout for danger.*

## DRAGONET

The electric blue stripes of this male become even brighter when he is courting a female. The blue and yellow dorsal fin sticks up like a flag in the shallow water where he swims.

*Small, simple eyes can detect changes in light and shade. They can tell day from night, and also see moving objects.*

## QUEEN SCALLOP

When a predator approaches this scallop, it swims jerkily through the water by clapping the two halves of its shell together.

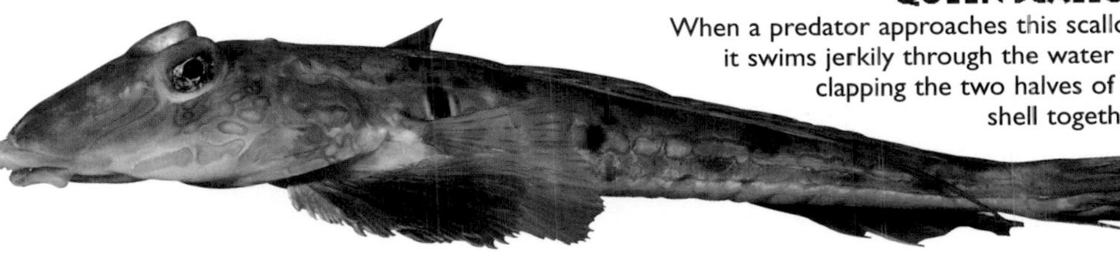

# CORAL REEF

Coral reefs only grow in sunny, shallow, tropical and subtropical seas. A reef is made up of different corals, all living side by side in separate colonies. Coral is made of the chalky outer skeletons of masses of polyps. These tiny animals look like sea anemones, and catch prey in their stinging tentacles. Many corals feed at night. By day, they withdraw into their chalky skeletons.

**RED SEA REEF**
Different kinds of coral grow in a variety of shapes. Brain corals are rounded clumps, fan corals form flattened sprays, and staghorn corals are branched.

*Branched staghorn coral*

## FRILLY SLUG

This sea slug feeds on other sea slugs. The frilly projections on its back help it to breathe.

## GIANT TRITON

This mollusk clings to any starfish it finds on the reef. It cuts into the starfish using its toothed radula like a saw, and eats the soft insides.

*The soft animal that creates this hard shell*

## CORAL HOME

A coral reef is a living home to many kinds of sealife. Fish, eels, skates, rays, sharks, and turtles swim around it looking for food or mates. Some creatures shelter in the crevices between the corals, hiding from predators.

## LINED SWEETLIPS

Sweetlip fish swim beside a reef, feeding on shrimps and other crustaceans from the sandy seabed.

*A mouth is ringed by tentacles.*

## ZOANTHARIA CORAL

These polyps are joined together at their fleshy bases. They do not produce a hard outer case, but grow in a creeping mat.

# LIFE ON THE SURFACE

**DIATOMS**
Photosynthesizing diatoms (single-celled algae) are abundant in coastal waters. Each has a minute silica shell, which fits together in two halves like a box.

The surface of the oceans teems with microscopic organisms and tiny animals: together, they are known as plankton. Microscopic algae use sunlight to photosynthesize, so they have to stay in the sunlit zone, the top 492 ft (150 m) of the sea. They are often called "the grass of the sea," because they are the basic fuel for many marine food chains.

**GROWING A STARFISH**
This free-swimming larva settles on a rock. At the unattached end, a minute starfish develops, then breaks away. It is only .039 in (1 mm) across!

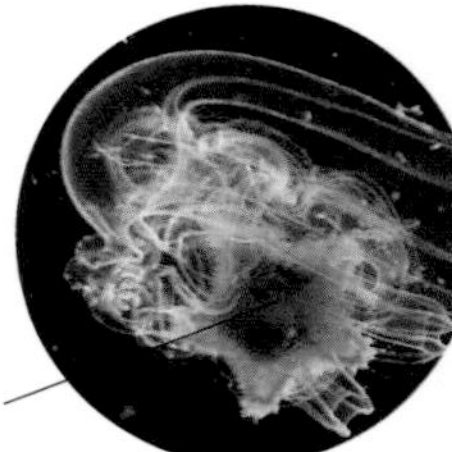

*A minute starfish develops inside the larva.*

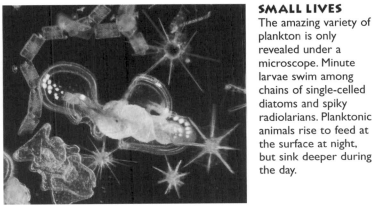

Plankton bloom

## PLANKTON BLOOM

When the weather is warm and there are plenty of nutrients dissolved in the sea, many forms of plankton multiply very quickly. There may be so much plankton that the water turns cloudy.

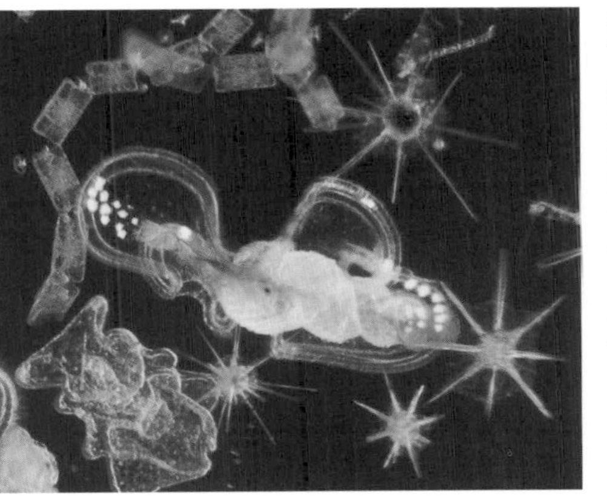

## SMALL LIVES

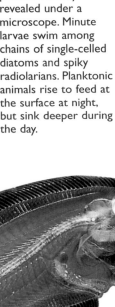

The amazing variety of plankton is only revealed under a microscope. Minute larvae swim among chains of single-celled diatoms and spiky radiolarians. Planktonic animals rise to feed at the surface at night, but sink deeper during the day.

## LARVAL FISH

After hatching, many kinds of young fish live among the plankton. Here they feed on the tiny organisms until they are big enough to swim away in a school.

## YOUNG NAUTILUS

This is a type of octopus that drifts in the open sea. As soon as a female hatches, two of its arms start to make the thin shell in which she will one day lay her eggs.

# SEA JOURNEYS

**SILVER EEL**
Brownish yellow adult eels live in freshwater rivers in Europe for 5 – 15 years. Then they turn black and silver, and swim nearly 3100 miles (5000 km), across the Atlantic Ocean to spawn in the Sargasso Sea.

Some fish, marine mammals, and reptiles travel thousands of miles every year. Often their long journeys are migrations from feeding areas to breeding grounds. Other fish swim long distances in their daily hunt for food, and to escape from predators trying to eat them. Some of these travelers use the oceanic currents that move huge masses of water through the oceans.

**GREEN SEA TURTLE**
Female turtles swim thousands of miles to return to their own nesting ground and breed. Green turtles living in Brazilian coastal waters make a 2800 mile (4500 km) journey to lay their eggs on Ascension Island.

*Flippers propel a turtle through the water.*

## MOVING TOGETHER

Tuna have torpedo-shaped bodies that slip speedily through the water. Schools of bigeye tuna travel through open water, hunting for food. They can swim very fast to avoid enemies.

## FLYING FISH

One way for a fish to escape from predators is to take to the air. A flying fish reaches a speed of about 40 mph (68 kph), before gliding on outstretched fins over the surface.

*Tuna in a school harmonize their movements and all move as one.*

## HUMPBACK WHALE

Humpback whales spend summers feeding in cold, food-rich, polar waters of the northern and southern hemispheres. In winter, they travel to the warm tropical seas, where the pregnant females give birth.

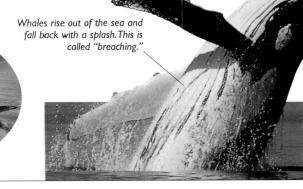

*Whales rise out of the sea and fall back with a splash. This is called "breaching."*

# IN THE DARK

The deepest parts of the sea floor are over 6 miles (10 km) deep. Sunlight reaches dimly down 0.62 miles (1 km). Below this it is completely dark. Food and mates are scarce and hard to find in the darkness. Many fish and invertebrates that live in the dark zone have light-producing organs on their bodies. Their sensitive eyes can detect these tiny traces of light.

**SUPER DIVER**
A sperm whale can dive nearly 2 miles (3 km), to feed on seabed sharks and deep-water squid. They can stay underwater for over an hour before coming up for air.

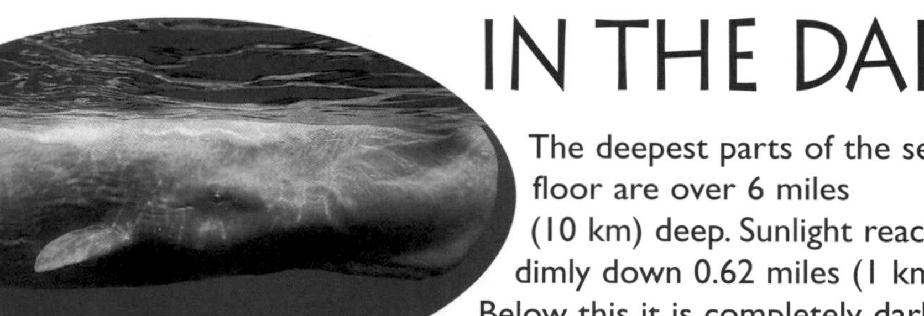

**DEEP-SEA ANGLERFISH**
Luminescent bacteria in the lure above the anglerfish's mouth attract prey nearby. Its stomach can stretch to hold a fish twice as big as itself.

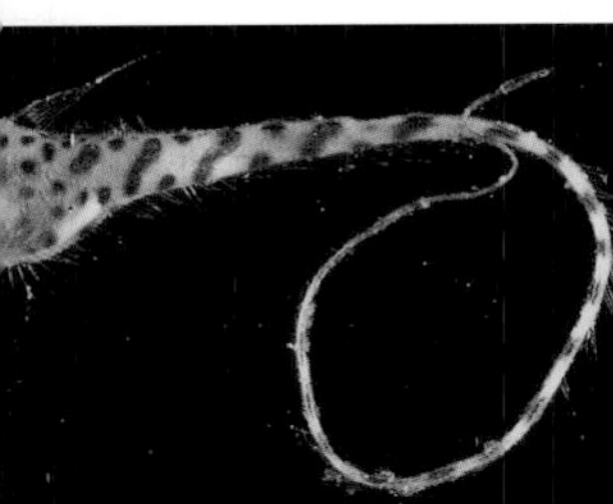

## RATFISH

Ratfish are one of the most common types of fish in deep water. The long, thin tail has no tail fin.

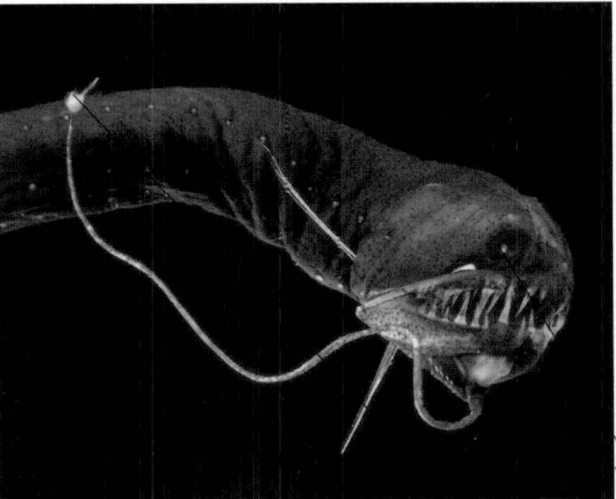

*Large eye*

*Photophores shine along the body. A separate glowing lure also attracts prey.*

## TEETH TRAP

A viper fish can open its jaws very wide indeed. Its long, needle-like teeth can pierce very slippery prey, which are swallowed whole.

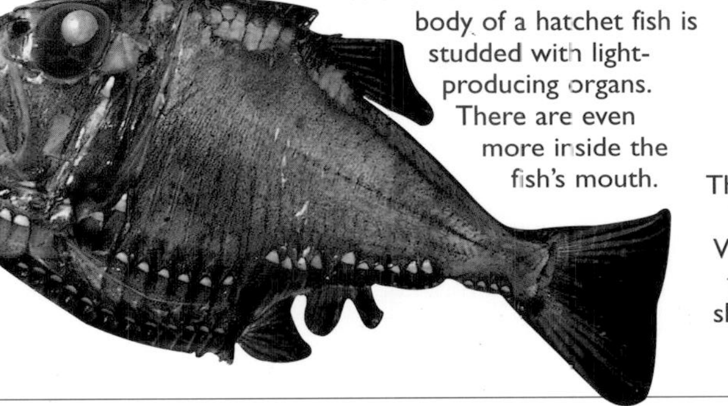

## LIGHTS ON

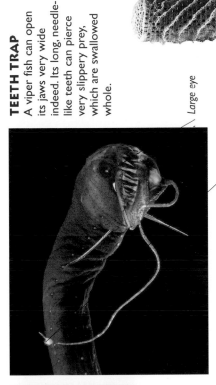

The lower half of the flattened body of a hatchet fish is studded with light-producing organs. There are even more inside the fish's mouth.

## VENUS FLOWER BASKET

This is the glassy skeleton of a Venus flower basket sponge. When alive, soft tissue covers this delicate frame. A pair of shrimp often lives inside this deep-water sponge.

# FILTER FEEDERS

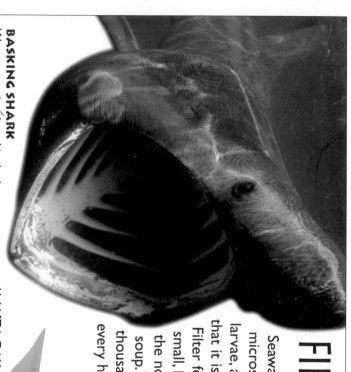

Seawater contains so much microscopic plankton, tiny larvae, and fragments of seaweeds that it is just like a thin soup. Filter feeders, both great and small, have methods of filtering the nourishment out of this soup. The largest feeders filter thousands of tons of water every hour!

**BASKING SHARK**
Water pours in when this shark opens its huge mouth. As the shark closes its mouth the water is forced out through gill rakers that trap all the plankton.

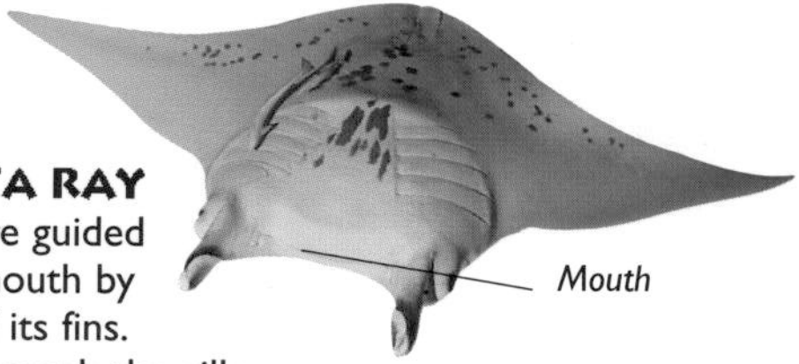

**MANTA RAY**
Small fish and plankton are guided into the manta's huge mouth by two armlike parts of its fins. Water filters out through the gills.

## SEA SQUIRTS

Tiny beating hairs draw water through a sea squirt. Plankton in the water sticks to a layer of mucus that passes into the gut.

## GIANT CLAM

This huge mollusk sieves seawater and consumes the organic particles it gathers. On the lip of its shell there are many raised, light-sensitive eyespots.

## VASE SPONGE

Water is drawn through tiny holes in the wall of the sponge. Plankton and particles of organic debris are trapped by cells lining the inside wall. Sieved water leaves from the top of the vase.

## FEATHER FANS

The feather worm has feathery tentacles that trap particles of dead seaweeds and sea animals. These are carried down into the worm's mouth by tiny hairs.

*Seaweed sometimes makes a thick forest of fronds; some are up to 330 feet (100 m) long.*

# SEA MEADOWS

Beds of seaweeds or sea grasses make underwater meadows that support a variety of animals. Brown seaweeds called kelps are attached to the seabed by very long stalks. Their fronds often have gas-filled bladders to keep them floating near the surface. They make an underwater forest. Many young seaweeds that settle on corals and rocks are eaten before they have a chance to grow large.

**MANATEE**
These placid, slow-moving sea cows munch the sea grasses in the shallow coastal waters of central America and Florida. They eat about 30 lb (15 kg) of sea grasses every day.

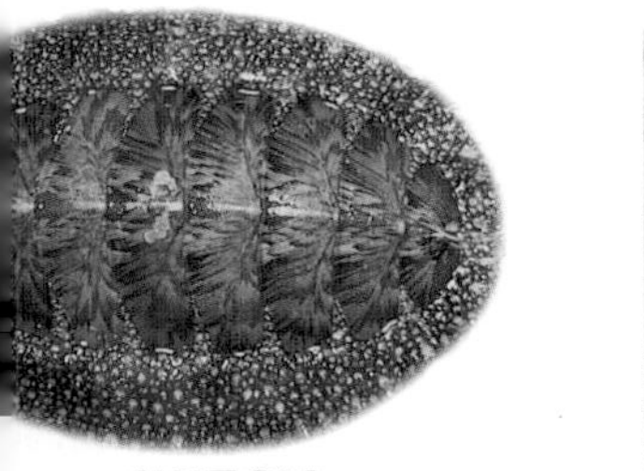

## CHITON

The armorlike shell of a chiton has eight plates and a fleshy rim. Chitons scrape juicy young seaweeds off rocks with a radula (tongue) covered with minute teeth.

## WALKING PIN CUSHION

This spiny sea urchin comes out at night to feed on algae growing on rocks and corals of a tropical reef. It scrapes the algae off rocks with teeth hidden beneath it.

## SEA HARE

Hidden by two wing-like flaps on the back of the sea hare is a tiny, thin shell. Sea hares feed on fronds of seaweed.

*Ear-shaped flaps*

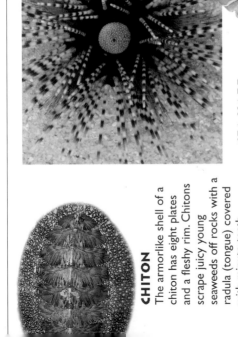

## BULLETHEAD PARROT FISH

The teeth of a parrot fish are joined together and look like a beak. The fish scrapes seaweeds off corals, sometimes crunching up bits of coral as well.

# DRIFTERS

Not all animals that live in the open sea are strong swimmers. Some drift along in the currents; others have a kind of sail and are blown along by the wind. Small animals latch onto driftwood or floating debris called flotsam. The fronds of floating seaweeds also provide shelter. If any of these animals drift close to land they may be stranded and perish.

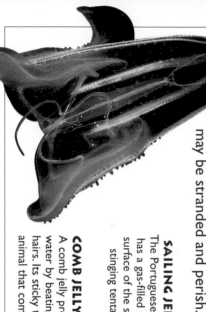

## SAILING JELLYFISH

The Portuguese man-of-war jellyfish has a gas-filled sac that floats on the surface of the sea. Dangling below it are stinging tentacles that trap and kill small crustaceans and fish.

## COMB JELLY

A comb jelly propels itself through the water by beating iridescent rows of tiny hairs. Its sticky tentacles grab any tiny animal that comes within its reach.

## HITCHHIKER

A goose barnacle attaches itself to boats or any floating driftwood by a long stalk. It captures small sea creatures in long hairy legs called cirri. A barnacle's protective shell develops from its skin.

*Minute bunches of hairs sprout from each jointed segment of the legs.*

## FISH OR WEED?

As well as living among floating seaweed, the anglerfish also lives on all sorts of other floating debris. It looks like just another piece of flotsam, but is a stealthy predator.

## FLOATING SEAWEED

Fronds of sargassum weed, torn away by storms from the eastern coast of the USA, grow in vast rafts which float in the Sargasso Sea.

*Hidden in the sargassum weed are small fish and crustaceans that the anglerfish entices with a lure above its mouth.*

# HUNTERS

All kinds of predators live in the sea. Catching enough to eat is difficult. Potential victims may be well-protected, very fast, or simply scarce. Every kind of hunter has its own strategy for catching food. Some of them rely on tentacles or pincers, but many rely on their speed and a lot of very sharp teeth.

**LONGTOM LOCKUP**
Some predators, such as the longtom, have interlocking teeth to prevent fish from escaping. Fish are fast swimmers, and they are covered with slimy mucus that makes them hard to catch.

**KILLER WHALE**
A killer whale often hunts with its family to catch fish, seals, seabirds, and even other whales. Prey too big to swallow whole is tossed into the air to be killed or snapped into pieces.

*Sharp, pointed teeth*

## A QUICK GRAB

A peacock mantis shrimp judges the distance to its prey perfectly before making a lightning strike. It grabs or impales its victim with its spiny front legs.

*Rows of extra teeth bend outward.*

## EXTRA TEETH

A shark catches and tears its prey apart with its sharp teeth. As its teeth break or fall out, they are replaced with another row of teeth from behind.

## FISHING FISH

The anglerfish lies in ambush, disguised as part of the seabed. It has a "fishing rod and lure" on top of its head to attract its prey.

*Lure*

## AMBUSH

A moray eel lies in wait under a rock ledge, its head sticking out, ready to strike.

# SWIMMING

Most fish swim by bending their bodies from side to side. Some fish use their fins while some sea mammals and turtles use their flippers to propel them along. Fins and flippers also help to steer, and act as brakes. High-speed swimming needs a streamlined shape like a tuna or a dolphin. Sea animals without fins swim by other means, including jet propulsion.

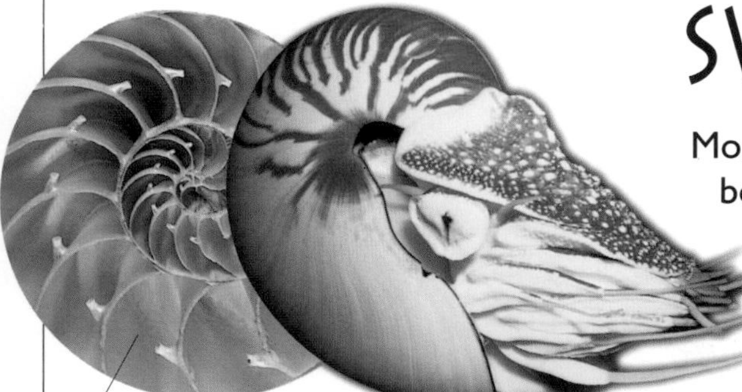

*New buoyancy chambers are added as the nautilus grows.*

**WATER PUMP**

A nautilus swims by jet propulsion – drawing water into itself, then forcing it out through a siphon. It controls its buoyancy by varying the amount of water in the hollow, air-filled chambers of its outer shell.

**S-SHAPED CURVE**

*The S-curve starts at the dogfish's head, then moves down its body.*

*The S-curve reaches the tail, which flicks to the right.*

## FLYING SWIM

A ray has very large pectoral fins. These flap up and down, so a ray looks as though it is flying through water.

## SCALES

Most fish have an outer layer of overlapping scales that are often thin and flexible. Scales grow as the fish grows. Glands in a fish's skin produce mucus that covers the fish in slime. The slime reduces friction and helps the fish to slip through the water.

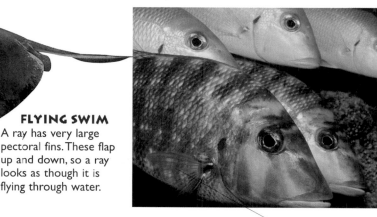

*Pectoral fins can be folded flat against the fish's body, or spread out to help it to steer.*

## COOL CURVES

Sharks such as this dogfish swim by bending their bodies in a series of S-shaped curves that thrust them forward. Their pectoral (side) fins steer them up and down and act as brakes.

*The tail flick propels the dogfish forward.*

*The body follows the head, bending to the left again in a continuous flowing movement.*

# CREEP & CRAWL

**BIGFOOT**
A limpet has one broad, flat foot. It slides over rocks as muscles in this foot contract and relax. If attacked, the limpet clamps down firmly against the rock.

Swimming and drifting are not the only ways of moving around the sea. Walking on the seabed or creeping over rocks and reefs may not be fast, but moving like this means that animals can stay under cover or close to shelter. Many sea animals that live close to the shore cling tightly to rocks as the tidal water surges in and out.

**LOBSTER LINES**
As soon as the water around the Florida coasts cools down in fall, spiny lobsters start to walk into deeper water. Up to 60 lobsters move forward in a single file, each lobster touching the one in front.

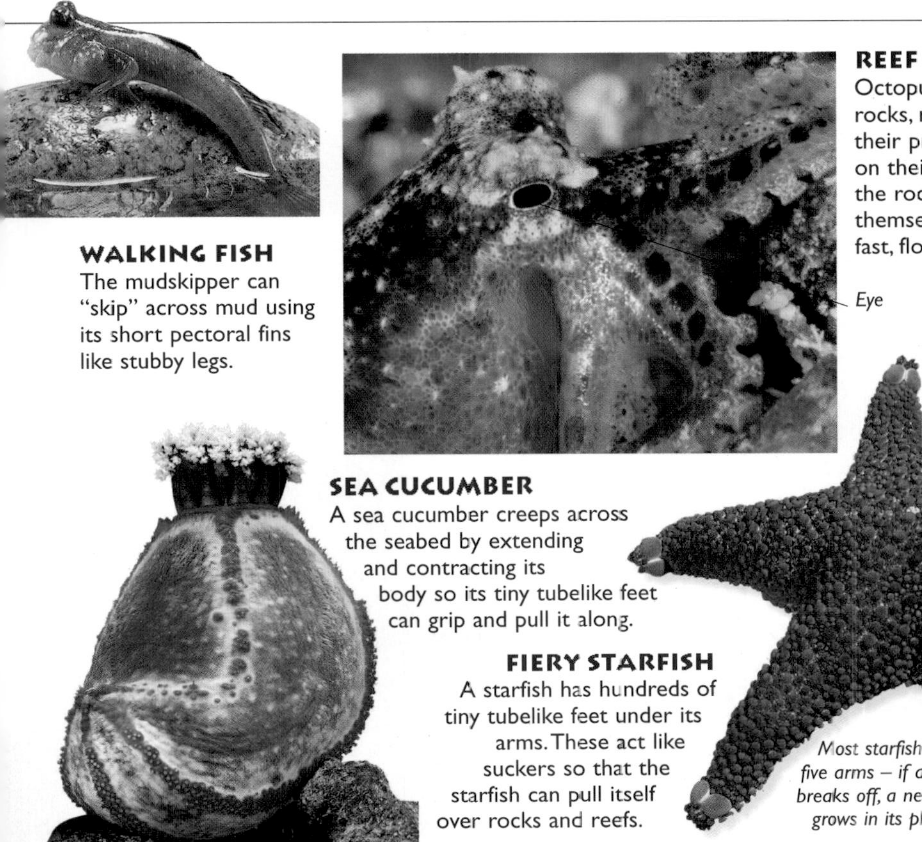

**WALKING FISH**
The mudskipper can "skip" across mud using its short pectoral fins like stubby legs.

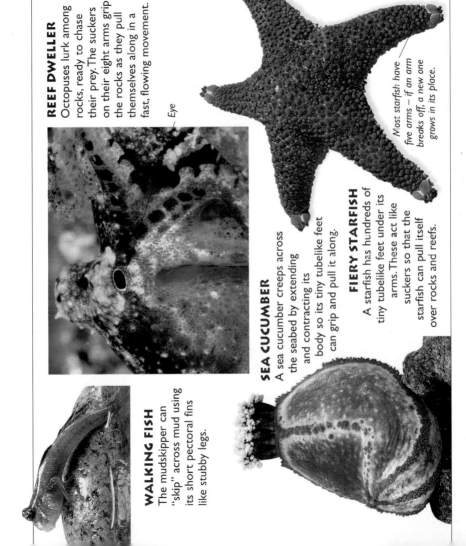

**REEF DWELLER**
Octopuses lurk among rocks, ready to chase their prey. The suckers on their eight arms grip the rocks as they pull themselves along in a fast, flowing movement.

*Eye*

**SEA CUCUMBER**
A sea cucumber creeps across the seabed by extending and contracting its body so its tiny tubelike feet can grip and pull it along.

**FIERY STARFISH**
A starfish has hundreds of tiny tubelike feet under its arms. These act like suckers so that the starfish can pull itself over rocks and reefs.

*Most starfish have five arms – if an arm breaks off, a new one grows in its place.*

# HIDING HOLES

**SHRIMP HOLE**
Lying hidden in an almost vertical burrow made in muddy sand, this mantis shrimp snatches any small prey that comes too close.

If an animal wants to hide on a sandy or muddy seabed, it has to burrow deep into the sediment. Some animals can burrow so quickly that they disappear almost instantly. Others make more permanent burrows or tunnels that become their home. These burrowers extend just part of their bodies into the water to catch food, to breathe, or to get rid of wastes.

**PIDDOCK HOLES**
The ends of a piddock's shell are strong enough to rasp away at soft rocks and excavate a really secure tunnel about 6 inches (15 cm) deep.

## BORING SPONGE

As this sponge grows, it dissolves the chalky coral of a reef to make pits and hollows in which to live. The sponge is sheltered, but its actions weaken the coral reef.

Feathery tentacles fan out to extract food and oxygen from the seawater.

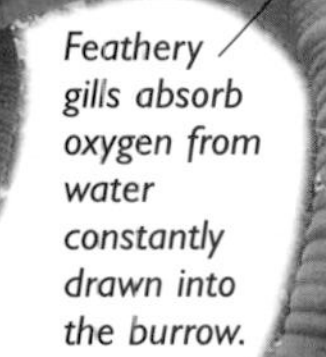

## CHRISTMAS TREE WORM

The feathery spirals that give this worm its name are filaments for feeding and breathing. The worm can withdraw entirely into its tube, which is embedded in living coral. Part of the worm forms a lid that closes the tube.

## UNDERGROUND SHELL

If a razor shell mollusk is uncovered, it uses its muscular foot to bury itself instantly in sand below low tide level. Usually only empty shells are found on the surface.

## U-TURN WORM

The lugworm lives in a U-shaped burrow lined with mucus. It swallows fine muddy sand, extracting food and leaving a worm cast. At low tide worm casts can be seen all over muddy shorelines.

Feathery gills absorb oxygen from water constantly drawn into the burrow.

# BUILDERS

Most marine mollusks and crustaceans make a protective chalky shell around their soft bodies. Crabs and their relatives secrete calcium salts and proteins from all over their skin that harden into a rigid case. Mollusks make their shells with just one part of their bodies, the mantle. Other animals use grains of sand to build themselves a home.

*A crab often eats its old shell so that the nutrients in it are not wasted.*

**CHANGING SHELLS**
Crab shells cannot grow. When a crab outgrows its shell, it molts. While its new shell hardens, the crab takes cover.

## HIDDEN PEARL

If a grain of sand lodges inside an oyster, the sand's sharp edges are covered with a smooth, lustrous shell, producing a pearl.

## MOLE COWRY

A layer of skin, the mantle, stretches up each side of its shell. When the animal retracts, its shell is too smooth to be gripped by a predator.

## SWAPPING HOMES

A hermit crab does not make its own shell. Instead, it uses an empty mollusk shell. As the crab grows it has to move into larger and larger mollusk shells.

## TRUMPET WORM

The body of this worm is long and soft. It uses mucus to cement large grains of sand into a hard case. The worm can withdraw inside its case and still feed by extending its tentacles.

## HORSE MUSSELS

Mollusks do not have to molt. They make their shells larger by adding new layers around the edge. Horse mussel shells can grow to be 8 inches (20 cm) long.

# SOUND WAVES

Clicking, squeaking, and booming sounds travel well underwater, and many fish and sea mammals use sounds to keep in touch. Sound can be picked up or "heard" in different ways. Fish pick up sounds through their gas-filled swim bladders, and the lateral lines that run along their sides. Sonar uses reflecting sounds (echoes) to find out about objects or prey. Sonar is used by dolphins, whales, and seals.

**BELUGA WHALES**
These whales "speak" in loud squeaks and squeals. In the past they were called sea canaries.

## NOISY FISH

Toadfish make a wide range of noises, from quiet growls to deafening croaks. They croak loudest when guarding their territory.

## DOLPHIN TALK

Dolphins find prey and avoid obstacles by using echolocation (sonar). They produce a series of rapid clicks and listen for the echo to bounce back. Dolphins are always making noises. They "speak" to each other in squeals.

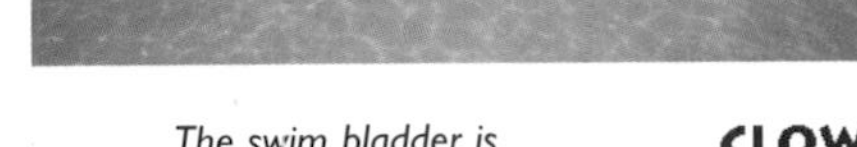


## HEARING AIDS

A fish's swim bladder keeps it buoyant so that it does not sink if it stops swimming. It also helps the fish to hear. Vibrations, including sound waves, are picked up by the lateral line canal and the swim bladder and transmitted to the fish's internal ears.

## CLOWN TRIGGERFISH

Some triggerfish make noises by vibrating muscles in their pectoral girdle. These noises are then amplified by the swim bladder.

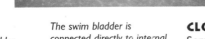

# LIGHT AND SHADE

Sunlight shining into the sea is soon absorbed by the water. The deeper you go, the less light there is. Even in the clearest seawater it is pitch dark below 3280 ft (1000 meters). Marine animals that live in the well-lit surface waters often rely on color. If fish in a school cannot see each other, the school breaks up. Many fish that live in deep water carry their own lights.

**FLASHLIGHT FISH**
Light-producing bacteria are gathered in organs below the fish's eyes. These flash on and off, making a brighter light than that of any other animal.

**HAMMERHEAD SHARK**
Having an eye at each side of its hammer-shaped head means that this shark cannot see straight ahead. It has to swing its head from side to side to look at things in front of it.

*The hammer-shaped head can "feel" the electrical field around its prey.*

## SUN SHADES

In shallow tropical seas the sunlight is often dazzling. The stingray has flaps which it extends to protect its eyes in bright light. This stops damage to the light-sensitive cells at the backs of its eyes.

*Flap to cover eye*

## PERISCOPE EYES

Eyes on the end of stalks give good all-around vision and allow the crab to stay in its hiding place.

*A ghost crab buries itself in the sand, leaving its eyes sticking out.*

*The eyes appear before the queen conch risks emerging from its shell.*

## POP EYES

The hatchet fish lives in the shadowy waters over 650 ft (200 meters) deep. Its bulging eyes are quick to detect prey drifting above it.

# COLOR

For fish and other sea creatures in shallow water or the brightly lit upper layers of the sea, color is used to send important messages. It can attract a mate, warn a predator of a bad taste so they do not attack, or trick a hungry fish into thinking that a small animal is really enormous.

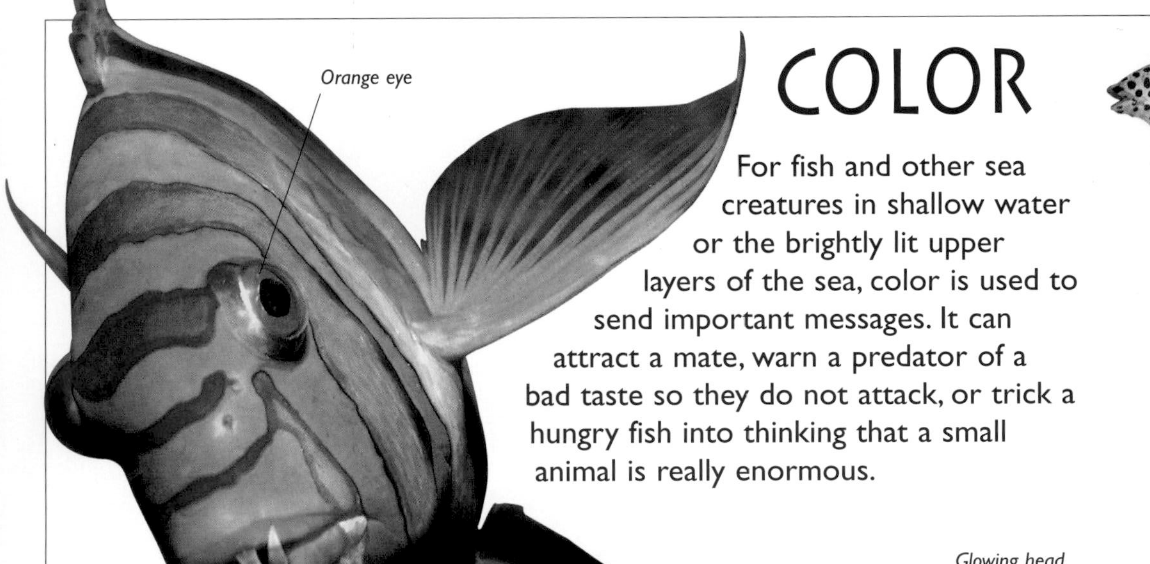


### HARLEQUIN TUSKFISH

Each vividly striped male vigorously defends its own territory. If another male intrudes, a tuskfish threatens it by displaying large, ferocious, blue teeth.

### QUICK CHANGE

Squid can change color very quickly. One may change color to blend in with its background or to reflect a change in its mood.

## EYE SPY

Two large, false eyespots on the side of this wrasse trick others into thinking it is the face of a much larger sea animal.

*Bright colors warn predators to stay away.*

## SECOND-HAND STINGS

These sea slugs feed on anemones that have stinging cells. These cells pass into the colorful breathing filaments on the slug's back. Here, they provide the slug with a second-hand stinging defense mechanism.

*This false eyespot makes the tail end of the fish look like its head.*

## WRONG END

The head of the forceps fish is invisible in the dappled light of a reef. A predatory fish may attack the wrong end of it, giving it time to escape.

## PRETTY BOY

A male boxfish looks as though it has just been freshly painted. Its brilliant pattern of spots is to impress the female boxfish.

# IN HIDING

Hiding from hungry predators is a way of avoiding their attention. When there is no hiding place, many creatures use camouflage to conceal themselves. Some turn the same color as the seabed or rocks around them; others look like a rock or a piece of seaweed. Predators also make use of camouflage to conceal themselves while they lie in wait for food.

*Each fin looks just like a lobed frond of seaweed.*

**LEAFY SEA DRAGON**
This sea horse lives in patches of seaweed growing close to the shore. It looks like a piece of torn kelp floating in the water.

*Bumpy barnacles*

**SPOT THE CRAB**
Many kinds of crab are masters of camouflage. This crab has exactly the same colors as the cockle shell on which it lives.

**BURIED IN SAND**
Flatfish such as flounder change color so that they blend in perfectly with the sand or pebbles. They lie half-buried and invisible on the seabed.

**FISH OR STONE**
Blotchy spots provide camouflage for this great flathead fish. It has no swim bladder, but lies like an oval stone on the bottom, ready to ambush a passing fish.

**PANTHER GROUPER**
The spots on this fish match the flickering light and shadows as sunshine filters through shallow water. They make the fish more difficult to see.

**MACKEREL**
Seen from below, these fish look pale against the sky. Viewed from above, their dark striped markings camouflage them against the deeper, darker water below.

# WEAPONS

Apart from hunting, most sea creatures only attack when they are in danger and need to defend themselves. Some fish have formidable weapons such as razor-sharp spines and blades. They may use these weapons when hunting, but they can also inflict serious injury to people and predators when they try to defend themselves.

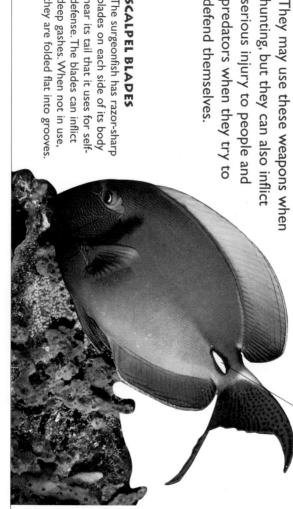

**SCALPEL BLADES**

The surgeonfish has razor-sharp blades on each side of its body near its tail that it uses for self-defense. The blades can inflict deep gashes. When not in use, they are folded flat into grooves.

## SWORD NOSE

The marlin swims into a school of fish at high speed, slashing with its long upper jaw. Then it eats all the injured fish that it can catch.

*A stingray lashes its tail to drive away a fish.*

## THE STING IN THE TAIL

The venomous, barbed spine on the upper side of a stingray's tail is only used for defense. Stingrays often lie buried in the sand in shallow water. Swimmers who step on them risk being stabbed by the sharp spine in the ray's tail.

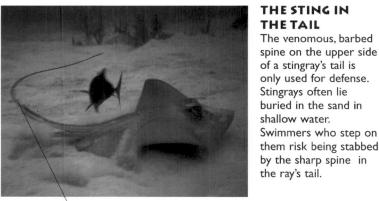

## SAWFISH

This long "saw" is armed with 15–30 pairs of sharp teeth. It is used to catch fish, and can also inflict serious wounds on larger predators such as whales.

*Bag of bait*

## GREAT WHITE SHARK

This shark feeds on dolphins, seals, and sea lions. It may attack swimmers if it mistakes them for its prey.

# IN THEIR OWN DEFENSE

*Each spine is tipped with a single crystal that has three cutting edges.*

A suit of armor can protect a small animal from being eaten by a larger predator. Another type of defense is a fearsome array of sharp spines to discourage even the hungriest attacker. Some animals seem overloaded with brittle defensive spines, and there are a few that can shock their enemies as well as their prey.

**CROWN OF THORNS STARFISH**
Anything coming into contact with this starfish is lacerated by its sharp spines. Small amounts of the starfish's toxic body fluids enter the cuts and cause great pain.

## HATPIN URCHIN

These long spines have serrated tips. If they stick into flesh, they snap off and inject painful venom.

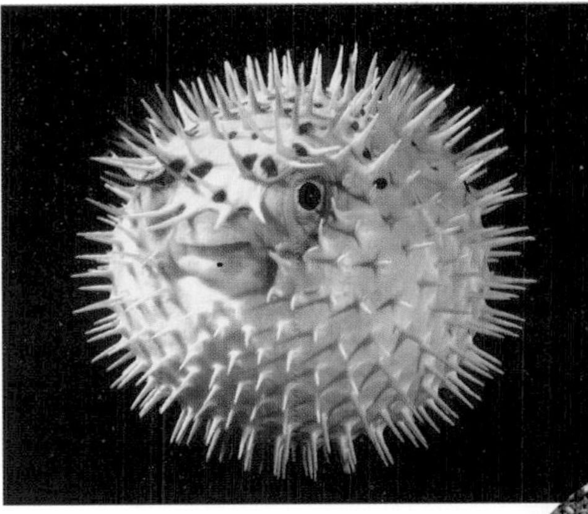

## A DANGEROUS BALL

When attacked, a puffer fish gulps water into its stretchy stomach until it is very round and two or three times its normal size. Spines that usually lie flat now stick out all over its body.

## ELECTRIC RAY

A large electric ray can produce a powerful electric shock up to 200 volts. This is enough to stun their prey, and to make a large predator think twice about attacking.

## LESSER WEAVER FISH

The weaver fish lies partly buried in the sand. If harmed or stepped on, spines on the dorsal fins and gill covers inject a painful dose of poison.

# MARINE VENOMS

A venom is a poisonous liquid that can be injected into another animal through teeth, spines, or stinging cells. There are many different kinds of venomous sea creatures, and they often have bright warning colors. They may use their venoms to overcome prey or to defend themselves against a predator. Some of them have venom strong enough to kill people.

**DEADLY WASP**
Thousands of stinging cells lie along the trailing tentacles of the tropical sea wasp. Humans that are stung may die unless they receive prompt medical treatment.

**CONE SHELL**
This mollusk has a proboscis that shoots out a sharp, venom-injecting dart. Fish-eating species have venom that kills fish instantly. It is also strong enough to kill an adult human.

## PAINFUL BEAUTY

The fin rays of the scorpion fish are drawn out into long spines. Inside each spine is a venom gland.

*The scorpion fish has venom that causes intense pain if it is injected into humans.*

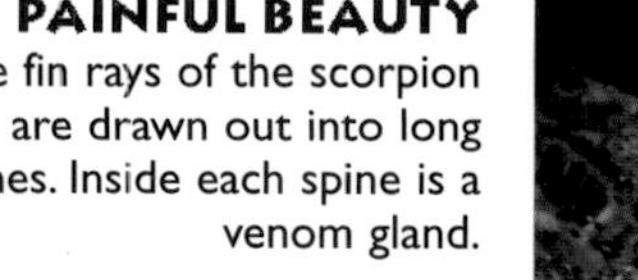

*Pale blue circles turn bright electric blue when the octopus is threatened.*

## BLUE RING OCTOPUS

This small octopus contains enough venom to kill 10 people. Its bite is painless, but venom flows into the wound from its salivary glands.

## OLIVE SEA SNAKE

This sea snake feeds on fish. Slender fangs inject a venom that kills a fish quickly before it can escape. Sea snake venom is powerful, but they rarely bite people.

*The snake hunts the seabed for prey.*

# PALS FOR LIFE

Strange partnerships have developed between many quite unrelated sea animals. Sometimes both partners profit from their friendship. Other times the gain seems one-sided. Some small fish and shrimp work as cleaners, keeping the bodies of larger fish free from parasites and from infections in their teeth and skin. How the cleaners themselves avoid being eaten is still unknown.

### A VENOMOUS RETREAT

Anemone fish shelter in the poisonous tentacles of a sea anemone. They are protected from the venom, which paralyzes other small fish.

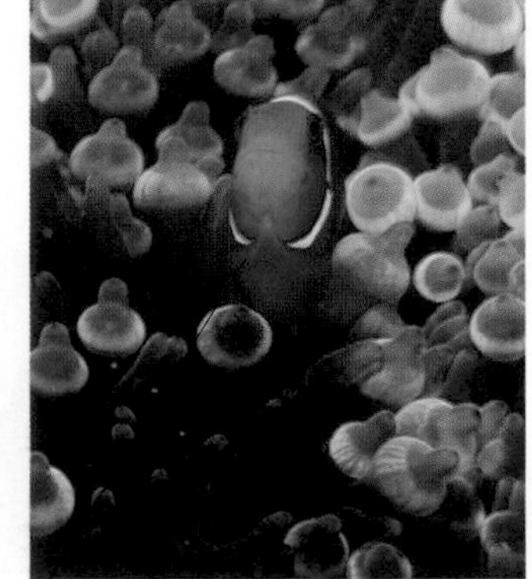

*Mucus covering this fish shields it from the anemone's stings.*

### CUNNING CRABS

Crabs use many tricks to make sure they survive. Some of them have struck up the most extraordinary partnerships.

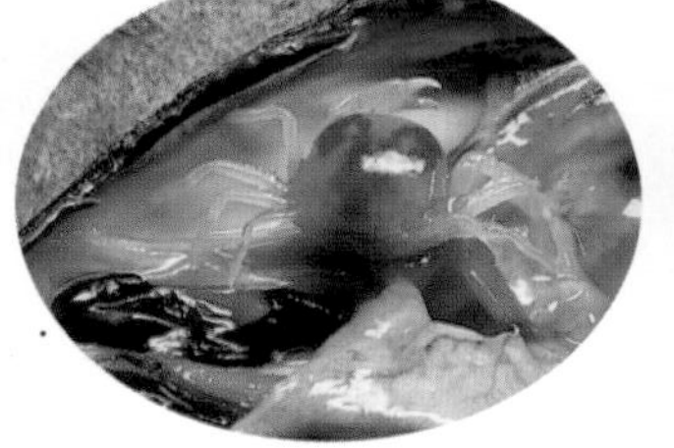

*Pea crabs live in mussel shells and steal some of the mussel's food. The mussel gets nothing in return.*

*A boxer crab picks up an anemone in each claw. It uses them to stun prey and sting predators.*

## DEEP CLEANING

This large grouper opens its mouth so that a little cleaner fish can swim in as far as its throat to pick off and eat any parasites and bits of food stuck between the grouper's teeth. The partnership is not permanent. Fish needing a brush-up gather at a cleaning station and invite a cleaner to start work.

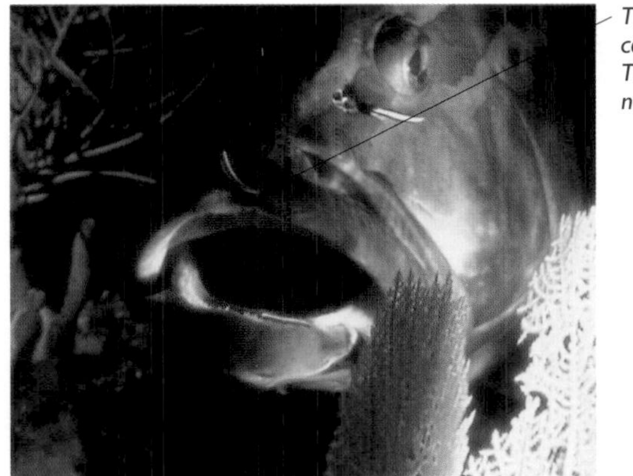

*The little fish, a brightly colored wrasse, is quite safe. The carnivorous grouper will not eat its small cleaner.*

## LITTLE HELPERS

Cleaner shrimp search the moray eel's skin, eating tiny parasites and cleaning infected wounds. This helps to keep the eel healthy, and gives the shrimp a meal.

*Sponge hat*

*This crab places sponges onto its hard shell to disguise it. The sponges share bits of the crab's food.*

# PAIRING UP

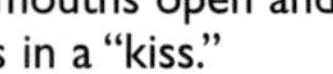

Finding a mate in the sea is not always easy. Some female fish that live in very deep water carry their tiny mate around with them! Other animals solve the problem by being both male and female at the same time. The rest rely on smell, color, or migration to a new area, often one rich in food, to find a mate.

**MATING WHELKS**
After a male and female whelk have mated, the female produces a mass of yolky eggs. These are stuck onto rocks or fastened to seaweed. Inside each egg, a tiny whelk develops.

*Grunts are colorful tropical fish. When not in pairs, they swim in schools.*

**A GRUNTING KISS**
Male fish often have to court females before they are allowed to mate. They may quiver their tails or make grunting noises by grinding their teeth. Pairs of courting grunts swim toward each other with their mouths open and touch lips in a "kiss."

## TRANSPARENT EGGS

These tube snout eggs are about to hatch. The female hides them under a piece of seaweed, but it is the male that guards them.

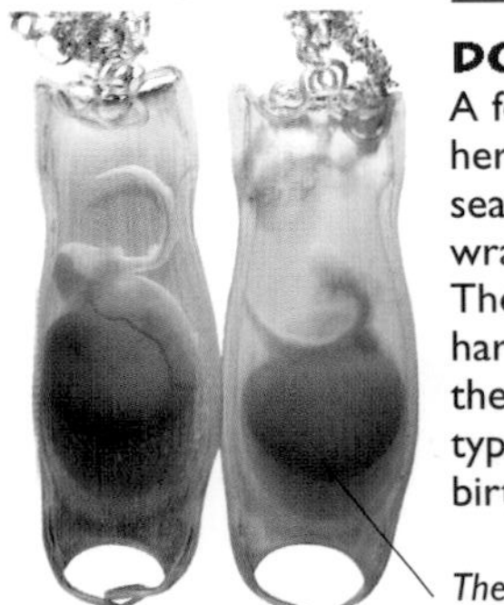

The embryo takes 8 – 9 months to develop before hatching.

## DOGFISH EGGS

A female dogfish lays her egg capsules in seaweed. Sticky threads wrap around the weed. These contract and harden, firmly anchoring the capsule. Many other types of shark give birth to live young.

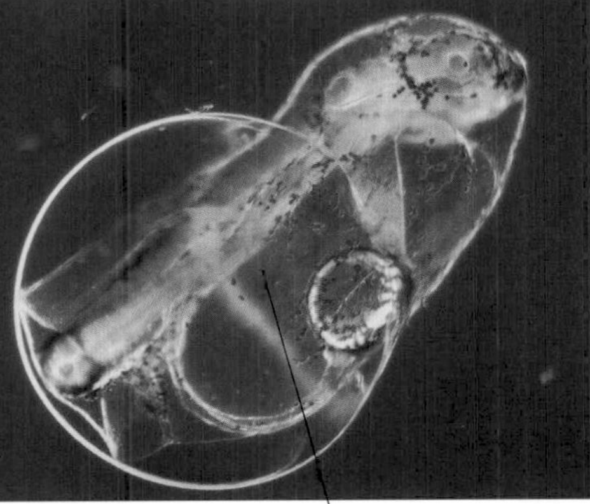

The tiny fish emerges with its yolk sac.

## FLOUNDER EGG

This flounder egg is hatching head first. The tiny hatchling stays near the surface of the water for a few weeks, then settles on the seabed.

## HATCHING OCTOPUS EGGS

A female octopus lays strings of eggs in a cave or rock crevice. She keeps them clean and aerated. Unable to feed herself while caring for the eggs, she then dies.

# MOMS AND DADS

**BANDED DAMSELFISH**
This fish is pushing a predatory starfish away from its eggs. It will keep them free of drifting debris, too.

There are two ways that sea creatures try to ensure their offspring will survive. Some produce hundreds, thousands, or even millions of eggs in the hope that a few will escape being eaten. Females that lay enormous quantities of eggs usually abandon them. Others lay far fewer eggs, but they take much better care of them. Sometimes the female guards her eggs.

Occasionally, the male is the caring parent, defending the eggs until they hatch.

**CARING DAD**
A male sea dragon has scales that form pockets along its tail. The female lays an egg in each pocket, and the male carries them until they hatch.

**VELVET CRAB**
A female crab keeps her eggs in a mass below her abdomen.

Humpback whales eat tiny fish and krill about 2 inches (5cm) long.

**HUMPBACK FAMILY**
A female whale gently nudges her newborn calf to the surface so it can breathe. She protects it and feeds it milk until it is large enough to look after itself.

**BEADLET BABIES**
The young of most anemones develop in the sea, but the beadlet incubates its eggs inside its body. When they are ready, the young appear from the beadlet's mouth.

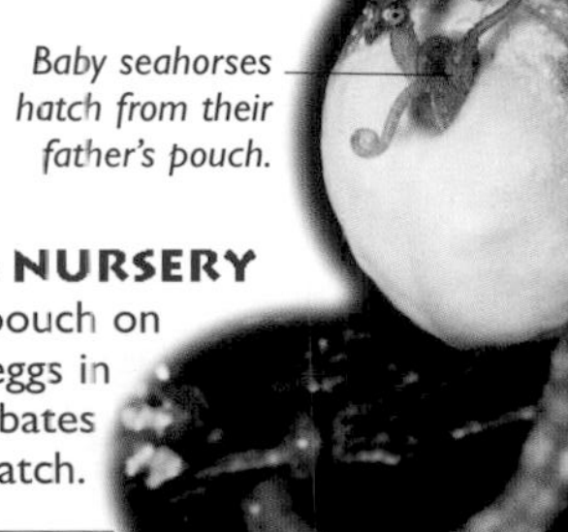

Baby seahorses hatch from their father's pouch.

**TRAVELING NURSERY**
A male sea horse has a pouch on his front. The female lays eggs in this pouch, and he incubates them until they hatch.

# INDEX

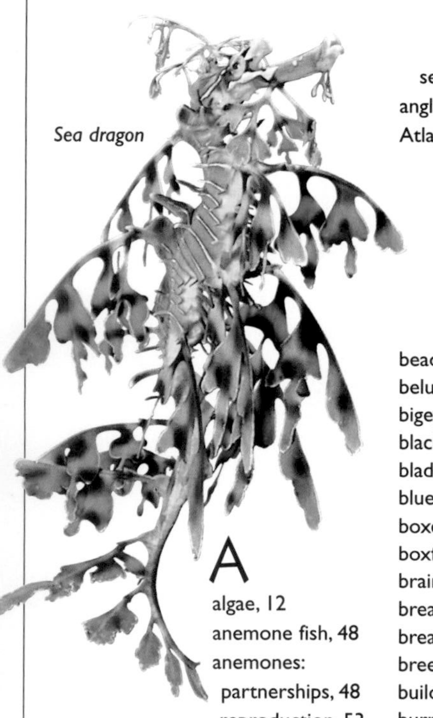

*Sea dragon*

## A



## B



## C

*Surgeonfish*

*Panther grouper*



# H, J, K



# L, M



# N, O, P

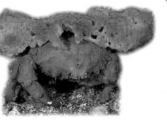

## Q, R



## S



*Sponge crab*

*Triggerfish*

## T



## V, W, Z